THE FACTS ON
CREATION
VS.
EVOLUTION

John Ankerberg
& John Weldon

HARVEST HOUSE PUBLISHERS
Eugene, Oregon 97402

Other books by
John Ankerberg and
John Weldon

The Facts on Abortion
The Facts on Angels
The Facts on Astrology
The Facts on the Faith Movement
The Facts on False Teaching in the Church
The Facts on Hinduism
*The Facts on Holistic Health
and the New Medicine*
The Facts on Homosexuality
The Facts on Islam
The Facts on the Jehovah's Witnesses
The Facts on Jesus the Messiah
The Facts on Life After Death
The Facts on the Masonic Lodge
The Facts on the Mind Sciences
The Facts on the Mormon Church
The Facts on the New Age Movement
The Facts on the Occult
The Facts on Rock Music
The Facts on Roman Catholicism
*The Facts on Self-Esteem, Psychology
and the Recovery Movement*
The Facts on Sex Education
The Facts on Spirit Guides
*The Facts on UFO's and
Other Supernatural Phenomena*

THE FACTS ON CREATION VS. EVOLUTION

Copyright © 1993 by The Ankerberg
   Theological Research Institute
Published by Harvest House Publishers
Eugene, Oregon 97402

ISBN 1-56507-152-2

Contents

Introduction

Section One
Evolution and Science

Section Two
Science and Creationism

Section Three
The Consequences
and Implications of
Evolutionary Theory

Introduction

1. Why is the issue of creation/evolution important?

The issue of creation/evolution* is important because, in the end, the subject of origins tells us who we are. Are we the product of the impersonal forces of matter, chance, and time—with all that implies? Or the result of special creation by an infinite, personal God—with all that implies? Because of its larger implications in areas such as science, religion, society, and morality, as well as its personal implications for individual identity and meaning in life, no one can deny the relevance of this subject.

We can also understand the importance of this subject if we briefly examine the influence of evolutionary theory in the last century. Sometimes powerful theories or ideologies can reach out and affect the lives of millions. They can influence personal philosophy, alter social and political institutions, and even direct the course of nations. Consider, for example, the ideologies of Marxism and Islam. The theory of evolution is one such materialistic ideology that has dramatically affected the world in which we live.

But if it turns out evolution is wrong, then everything it has impacted may have been affected in a prejudicial or even harmful way.

2. How influential is the theory of evolution?

In the history of mankind, few theories have had the impact that evolution has. The famous evolutionary zoologist Ernst Mayr of Harvard University observed in 1972 that evolution was coming to be regarded as "perhaps the most fundamental of all intellectual revolutions in the history of mankind."[1] The definitive modern biography by James Moore, *Darwin: The Life of a Tormented Evolutionist*, points out that Darwin, "More than any modern thinker—even Freud or Marx...has transformed the way we see ourselves on the planet."[2] Wendell R. Bird is a prominent Atlanta attorney and Yale Law School graduate who argued the major creationist case on the issue of creation/evolution before the U.S. Supreme Court. In his impressive criticism

---

* The term *evolution* is used in reference to the general theory that all life on earth has evolved from nonliving matter and has progressed to more complex forms with time; hence, "macroevolution" and not "microevolution" or minor changes within species illustrated in crossbreeding (e.g., varieties of dogs).

of evolutionary theory, *The Origin of Species Revisited*, he observes of *The Origin of Species*, "That single volume has had a massive influence not only on the sciences, which increasingly are built on evolutionary assumptions, but on the humanities, theology, and government."[3]

In his *Mankind Evolving* eminent geneticist Theodosius Dobzhansky, who is regarded as among the world's greatest evolutionists, points out that the publication of Darwin's book in 1859 "marked a turning point in the intellectual history of mankind" and "ushered in a new understanding of man and his place in the universe."[4] He reflects that even a hundred years after Darwin "the idea of evolution is becoming an integral part of man's image of himself. The idea has percolated to much wider circles than biologists or even scientists; understood or misunderstood, it is a part of mass culture."[5]

Molecular biologist Michael Denton points out the dramatic influence of this increasingly dominant theory in disciplines outside the natural sciences:

> The twentieth century would be incomprehensible without the Darwinian revolution. The social and political currents which have swept the world in the past eighty years would have been impossible without its intellectual sanction.... The influence of evolutionary theory on fields far removed from biology is one of the most spectacular examples in history of how a highly speculative idea for which there is no really hard scientific evidence can come to fashion the thinking of a whole society and dominate the outlook of an age.[6]

> Today it is perhaps the Darwinian view of nature more than any other that is responsible for the agnostic and skeptical outlook of the twentieth century.... [It is] a theory that literally changed the world....[7]

Indeed, it is how an individual views his origin, his ultimate beginning, that to a great extent conditions his worldview, the decisions he makes, and even his general lifestyle.

Thus, Julian Huxley observed that evolution is far more than a scientific theory: "Our present knowledge indeed forces us to the view that the whole of reality *is* evolution—a single process of self-transformation."[8] This is why Dobzhansky could emphasize: "Evolution comprises all the stages of the development of the universe: the cosmic, biological, and human or cultural developments. Attempts to restrict the concept of evolution to biology are gratuitous. Life is a product of the evolution of inorganic nature, and man is a product of the evolution of life."[9] Writing in *Scientific American*, Ernst Mayr observed that "man's world view today is dominated by [evolution]...."[10] Thus, leading ecologist Rene Dubois observed in *American Scientist*: "Evolutionary concepts are applied also to social institutions and to the arts. Indeed, most political parties, as well as schools of theology, sociology, history, or arts, teach these concepts and make them the basis of their doctrines."[11]

As if to symbolize this worldwide influence of evolution, the U.N. itself has been dominated by an evolutionary perspective. For example, Sir Julian Huxley was UNESCO's first Director-General. In its formative years, UNESCO's basic philosophy also served to guide the United Nations. In that connection Huxley observed in *The Humanist*, "It is essential for UNESCO to adopt an evolutionary approach. ... The general philosophy of UNESCO should, it seems, be a scientific world humanism, global in extent and evolutionary in background.... Thus the struggle for existence that underlies natural selection is increasingly replaced by conscious selection, the struggle between ideas and consciousness."[12] As United Nations Assistant Secretary-General Robert Muller, a promoter of certain New Age ideals around the world, once observed: "I believe the most fundamental thing we can do today is to believe in evolution."[13]

But what if evolution turns out to be false? And further, as we will discuss in detail later, belief in evolution can have unexpected consequences. It did for Darwin. Few people realize the extent of Darwin's own doubts over his theory, a theory which he confessed was "grievously hypothetical."[14] As he wrestled with the consequences of theism versus materialism, he suffered physically, mentally, and spiritually.[15] To the end of his life, his attempt to escape God by defending what he once termed "the devil's gospel" produced an internal warfare that brought Darwin pain and anguish, at times even making him irrational.[16]

It is hardly surprising. Darwin was defending the incredible idea that universal life originated entirely from lifeless matter or at least from some primitive germ. Solely by chance. Yet even he admitted he could find no real evidence for this theory.[17] And most of the scientists of his own day could not accept his theory on scientific grounds.[18] Evolution gained stature within 30 years not because of compelling evidence on its behalf, but because the American intellectual climate had already been prepared for a shift away from theism and supernaturalism to humanism and naturalism.[19] Indeed, the world jumped at Darwin because it was ready for Darwin.

Significantly, in the subsequent 140 years since Darwin formulated his theory, modern evolutionary scientists still have not successfully answered their critics. The fossil record remains entirely deficient of proven intermediate links, sufficient time still does not exist for evolution to occur, no credible mechanism of evolutionary change has yet been advanced, and mathematical probabilities and scientific laws such as those dealing with biogenesis, thermodynamics, and information science make chance evolution an impossibility.[20] As molecular biologist Michael Denton observes: "Neither of the two fundamental axioms of Darwin's macroevolutionary theory [i.e., 1) the evolutionary continuity of nature linking all life forms on a continuum leading back to a primal origin, and 2) the adaptive design of life resulting from blind random processes] have been validated by one single empirical discovery or scientific advance since 1859."[21]

So why was evolution ever accepted in the first place? In the following pages we will seek to answer that question as well as determine the credibility of this theory and some of the reasons for its influence.

Section One
Evolution and Science

3. What is science? Is the theory of evolution properly scientific?

There exists many popular misunderstandings concerning the nature of science. Philosopher of science Dr. J.P. Moreland discusses some of these misconceptions and observes that even "scientists today, in contrast to their counterparts in earlier generations, are often ill equipped to define science, since such a project is philosophical in nature."[22] In fact, Moreland cites several standard definitions of science given in such texts as *College Physics*, *Biological Science*, *Webster's New Collegiate Dictionary* as well as Judge William R. Overton's definition of science in the decision against creationism in the famous creation science trial in Little Rock, Arkansas, December 1981. He observes that none of these definitions is adequate.[23]

The interaction of science and philosophy is a complex one. There is no universally accepted clear-cut definition of what science is. We are on safer ground if we define science in a general way, noting its methodology, in other words, the scientific method. For our purposes, the *Oxford American Dictionary* (1982) definition of science, though incomplete, is adequate: "A branch of study which is considered either with a connected body of *demonstrated truths* or with *observed facts* systematically classified and more or less colligated and brought under *general laws*, and which includes *trustworthy methods* for the discovery of *new truth* within its own domain." Scientific work involves things like observation, formulating a hypothesis, experimental testing to repeat observations, predictability, control, etc.:

> One applies the scientific method by first of all observing and recording certain natural phenomena. He then formulates a generalization (scientific hypothesis) based upon his observations. In turn, this generalization allows him to make predictions. He then tests his hypothesis by conducting experiments to determine if the predicted result will obtain. If his predictions prove true, then he will consider his hypothesis verified. Through continual confirmation of the predictions [e.g., by himself and other parties] the hypothesis will become a theory, and the theory, with time and tests, will graduate to the status of a [scientific] law.[24]

What this generally accepted definition of science and the scientific method indicates is that while evolution utilizes the scientific method, evolutionary theory itself is not ultimately scientific because evolution has few, if any, "demonstrated truths" or "observed facts." Microevolution or strictly limited change within species can be demonstrated but this has nothing to do with evolution as commonly understood. After citing evolutionists who confess that evolution is not scientifically provable, Wysong observes, "Evolution is not a formulation of the true scientific method. They [these scientists] realize evolution means the initial formation of unknown organisms from unknown chemicals produced in an atmosphere or ocean of unknown composition under unknown conditions, which organisms have then climbed an unknown evolutionary ladder by an unknown process leaving unknown evidence."[25]

In other words, to the extent that science hinges upon demonstrated truths or observed facts, evolutionary theory is not science; rather it is a philosophy. A.E. Wilder-Smith, who holds three earned doctorates in science, observes:

> As Kerkut has shown [in his *Implications of Evolution*], Neodarwinian thought teaches seven main postulates. Not one of these seven theses can be proved or even tested experimentally. If they are not supported by experimental evidence, the whole theory can scarcely be considered to be a *scientific* one. If the seven main postulates of Neodarwinism are experimentally untestable, then Neodarwinism must be considered to be a philosophy rather than a science, for science is concerned solely with experimentally testable evidence.[26]

4. Should evolution be claimed as an established scientific fact?

Evolution continues to be set forth as an *established* fact by the scientific community, but principally because of the materialistic, naturalistic viewpoint that pervades the scientific world.[27]

Pierre-Paul Grasse, the renown French zoologist and past president of the French Academy of Sciences, states in his *Evolution of Living Organisms*: "Zoologists and botanists are nearly unanimous in considering evolution *as a fact* and not a hypothesis. I agree with this position and base it primarily on documents provided by paleontology, i.e., the [fossil] history of the living world."[28] Theodosius Dobzhansky, who, according to another leading evolutionist, Steven J. Gould of Harvard, is "the greatest evolutionist of our century,"[29] asserts in his award-winning text, *Mankind Evolving*, "The *proofs of evolution* are now a matter of elementary biology.... In Lamark's and Darwin's times evolution was a hypothesis; in our day it is *proven*."[30] World famous scientist George Gaylord Simpson, distinguished professor of vertebrate paleontology at the Museum of Comparative Zoology at Harvard, emphasizes in *The Meaning of Evolution*, "*Ample proof* has been repeatedly presented and is available to anyone who really wants to know the truth. ...In the present study the *factual truth* of organic evolution is taken as *established*...."[31]

Carl Sagan is a distinguished Cornell University astronomer and Pulitzer prize-winning author. He is perhaps best known as the host and co-writer of the *Cosmos* television series, seen in 60 countries by approximately 3 percent of all people on earth. The hardcover edition of *Cosmos* was on the

New York Times bestseller list for 70 weeks and may be the bestselling science book in the English language in the twentieth century. In this book, Sagan simply states, "Evolution is *a fact*, not a theory."[32]

On the other hand, creationists and other non-evolutionary scientists argue that evolution cannot logically be considered factual apart from any real evidence: "All the hard data in the life sciences show that evolution is not occurring today, all the real data in the earth sciences show it did not occur in the past, and all the genuine data in the physical sciences show it is not possible at all. Nevertheless, evolution is almost universally accepted as a fact in all the natural sciences."[33] One can only ask, "Why?" Again, simply because evolution is more philosophy than science. What does this mean?

Consider the comments of the Canadian scholar Arthur C. Custance (Ph.D. anthropology) and author of the ten-volume *Doorway Papers*. He is a member of the Canadian Physiological Society, a fellow of the Royal Anthropological Institute, and a member of the New York Academy of Sciences.

In "Evolution: An Irrational Faith" he observes,

> Virtually all the fundamentals of the orthodox evolutionary faith have shown themselves to be either of extremely doubtful validity or simply contrary to fact. . . . So basic are these erroneous [evolutionary] assumptions that the whole theory is now largely maintained *in spite of* rather than *because of* the evidence. . . . As a consequence, for the great majority of students and for that large ill-defined group, 'the public,' it has ceased to be a subject of debate. Because it is both incapable of proof and yet may not be questioned, it is virtually untouched by data which challenge it in any way. It has become in the strictest sense *irrational*. . . . Information or concepts which challenge the theory are almost never given a fair hearing. . . .[34]

In fact, in the opinion of this esteemed scholar, "Evolutionary philosophy has indeed become *a state of mind*, one might almost say a kind of mental prison rather than a scientific attitude. . . . To equate one particular interpretation of the data with *the data itself* is evidence of mental confusion. . . . The theory of evolution . . . is detrimental to ordinary intelligence and warps judgment."[35]

He concludes, "In short, the premises of evolutionary theory are about as invalid as they could possibly be. . . . If evolutionary theory was strictly scientific, it should have been abandoned long ago. But because it is more philosophy than science, it is not susceptible to the self-correcting mechanisms that govern all other branches of scientific enquiry."[36]

5. Are scientists always objective?

Scientists are people. Thus, science has its share of ambition, suppression of truth, prejudice, greed, plagiarism, manipulation of data, etc. This is proven by Tel Aviv Medical School's professor of urology Alexander Kohn in his *False Prophets: Fraud and Error in Science and Medicine* (1986) and by Broad and Wade's *Betrayers of the Truth: Fraud and Deceit in the Halls of Science* (1982).

The biases many scientists have against scientific creationism can be seen through contemporary examples.

When one of the greatest thinkers of modern times, Mortimer J. Adler of the University of Chicago, referred to evolution as a "popular myth," Martin Gardner actually included him in his study of quacks and frauds in *Fads and Fallacies in the Name of Science*.[37] As philosopher and historian Dr. Rousas Rushdoony observes, "To question the myth or to request proof is to be pillared as a modern heretic and fool."[38]

Consider the case of Dr. A.E. Wilder-Smith. Smith earned three doctorates in science. His noteworthy academic career spans 40 years, including the publication of more than 100 scientific papers and more than 40 books which have been published in 17 languages. Before discussing his own case, he illustrates with two others where eminent scientists have been silenced because they dared question evolutionary theory:

> Over and above this, the situation is such today that any scientist expressing doubts about evolutionary theory is rapidly silenced. Sir Fred Hoyle, the famous astronomer, was well on his way to being nominated for the Nobel Prize. However, after the appearance of his books expressing mathematically based doubts as to Darwinism, he was rapidly eliminated. His books were negatively reviewed and no more was heard about his Nobel Prize. The case of the halo dating methods developed by Robert V. Gentry tell a similar story. Gentry gave good evidence that the earth's age, when measured by the radiation halo method using polonium, might not be so great as had been thought

when measured by more conventional methods. A postulate of this type would have robbed Darwinism of its main weapon, namely long time periods. Gentry lost his research grants and job at one sweep.

It is by such methods, often bordering on psychoterror, that the latter day phlogiston theory (Neodarwinism) still manages to imprint itself in pretty well all scientific publications today. I myself gave the Huxley Memorial Lecture at the Oxford Union, Oxford University, on February 14, 1986. My theses were well received even by my opponents in the debate following the lecture. But I have been to date unable to persuade any reputable scientific journal to publish the manuscript. The comment is uniformly that the text does not fit their scheme of publications.

I recently (December 1986) received an enquiry from the Radcliffe Science Library, Oxford, asking if I had ever really held the Huxley Memorial Lecture on February 14, 1986. No records of my having held the lecture as part of the Oxford Union debate could be found in any library nor was the substance of this debate ever officially recorded. No national newspapers, radio or TV station breathed a word about it. So total is the current censorship on any *effective* criticism of Neodarwinian science and on any genuine alternative.[39]

As Dr. Jerry Bergman and others have documented, there are thousands of cases of discrimination against creationists—of competent science teachers being fired merely because they taught a "two model approach" to origins; of highly qualified science professors being denied tenure because of their refusal to declare their faith in evolution; of students' doctoral dissertations in science rejected simply because they supported creation; of students being expelled from class for challenging the idea that evolution is a fact.[40]

Prominent lawyer Wendell R. Bird, author of *Origin of Species Revisited*, observes that "most of higher education is dogmatic and irrationally committed to affirm evolution and to suppress creation science, not on the basis of the scientific evidence but in disregard of that evidence." He correctly refers to the "intolerance," "hysteria," and "unfairness" of the evolutionary establishment and to the "intolerable denials of tenure, denials of promotion, denials of contract renewals, denials of earned degrees, denials of admission into graduate programs, and other discrimination against that minority that disagrees with the prevailing dogmaticism and dares affirm creation science...."[41]

In doing research for *The Criterion*, Dr. Bergman interviewed more than 100 creationists who had at least a master's degree in science, the majority with a Ph.D. degree—among them Nobel prize winners and those with multiple doctorates in science. "Nevertheless, all, without exception, reported that they had experienced some discrimination...some cases were tragic in the extent, blatancy and consequences of the discrimination, even including death threats."[42]

The hypocrisy in all this seems evident enough. The evolutionary establishment demands freedom of expression for itself but refuses this to its opposition. As Dr. Thomas Dwight of Harvard observed, "The tyranny in the matter of evolution is overwhelming to a degree of which the outsider has no idea."[43] In our colleges and universities today, the Christian faith can be ridiculed all day long, the Constitution criticized, marriage degraded, and morality questioned, but the theory of evolution is somehow sacrosanct. Chicago University's professor Paul Shoray observed, "There is no cause so completely immune from criticism today as evolution."[44]

Even the head of the science department at an Ivy League university tore out an article in *Systematic Zoology* because it was critical of natural selection. When confronted he said, "Well of course I don't believe in censorship in any form, but I just couldn't bear the idea of my students reading that article."[45]

6. Why do materialistic scientists accept evolution?

There is a tacit assumption that science, even in matters concerning origins, must be naturalistic. It's defined this way. Upon individual reflection, materialistic scientists today may find it difficult to imagine that all life on earth originated by chance from dead matter, yet many find the idea of divine creation far more difficult. For these scientists evolution must be accepted as a philosophical necessity regardless of the scientific evidence.

But how wise is this approach? Ideally, science is to involve a search for truth in an objective manner wherever that search happens to lead. If the scientific *facts* really do point to creation, then this may at least be conceded, whether or not it is personally accepted. Consider the comments of the eminent space scientist Dr. Wernher von Braun, developer of the Saturn rocket and the pioneer behind the space shuttle. He is only one of many scientists convinced that good science and belief in a Creator go hand in hand:

> Manned space flight is an amazing achievement, but it has opened for mankind thus far only a tiny door for viewing the awesome reaches of space. An outlook through this peephole at the vast mysteries of the universe should only confirm our belief in the certainty of its Creator.
>
> I find it as difficult to undertand a scientist who does not acknowledge the presence of a superior rationality behind the existence of the universe as it is to comprehend a theologian who would deny the advances of science. And there is certainly no scientific reason why God cannot retain the same relevance in our modern world that He held before we began probing His creation with telescope, cyclotron, and space vehicles.[46]

In *Why Scientists Accept Evolution*, Drs. Clark and Bales document that "men often accept evolution because the only alternative is creation by God."[47] Put another way, if evolution is *not* true, materialistic scientists would be uncomfortable with the implications because they would be confronted with evidence for the existence of God. Because they are unwilling to accept a concept of divine creation, "They frame whatever hypotheses are necessary to sustain a hypothesis of evolution."[48]

Thus, many frank scientists have confessed that the reasons behind their belief in evolution are primarily philosophical, not scientific. Nowhere is this better illustrated than by citing the Nobel prize-winning biologist of Harvard University, Dr. George Wald, who once confessed, "One only has to contemplate the magnitude of this task to concede that the spontaneous generation of a living organism is impossible. Yet here we are—as a result, I believe, of spontaneous generation"[49] (see footnote 49). But earlier, Dr. Wald stated what evidently was the real problem:

> The reasonable view was to believe in spontaneous generation; the only alternative, to believe in a single, primary act of supernatural creation. There is no

third position. For this reason many scientists a century ago chose to regard the belief in spontaneous generation as a philosophical necessity.... Most modern biologists, having viewed with satisfaction the downfall of the spontaneous generation hypothesis, yet unwilling to accept the alternative belief in special creation, are left with nothing.[50]

Another scientist, G. Fana, confessed, "Let us admit without further preamble: the success attained by the theory of evolution is not due primarily to its self-evident character, for even the most generally admitted facts cannot always be reconciled with it, but rather to the sympathy of the scientific world for the 'dogma' of scientific materialism."[51]

Scientist Louis T. More made the following confession: "When, however, we examine these causes for our belief [in evolution] we find that, accepting our desire to eliminate special creation and, generally, what we call the miraculous, most of them can be considered only as secondary reasons to confirm a theory already advanced."[52]

7. How is it possible for so many scientists to be wrong in their belief in evolution?

The history of science reveals many instances where the majority of scientists have been convinced as to a particular theory and yet have been wrong. Further, when it comes to the discussion of the creation/evolution issue, many scientists today simply seem to be closed minded. Why? Because modern science is committed to the ideology of evolution and any time a philosophical commitment to a particular ideology exists, there is typically a reluctance to consider alternate viewpoints.

Indeed, there are several reasons explaining why scientists who accept evolution can be wrong. Among them we mention four.

1. A false theory can be accepted by mistakenly assuming there are no legitimate theories to replace it.

Dr. Wilder-Smith observes that when the modern scientific establishment adheres to evolutionary theory, it is "certainly not because experimental evidence encourages the establishment to do so."[53] He explains that a commitment to materialism is the problem. Thus,

There exists at present no other *purely scientific* alternative which postulates a purely scientific materialistic basis for biogenesis and biology. To repeat, there is at present no *purely scientific alternative to Darwin*. Creationism, being religious, is of little use to the materialistic thought of today. It is simply an irrelevant subject worthy only of ridicule.... Scientists whose upbringing and education are Darwinian and therefore naturalistic, have for this reason no real alternative to Darwinism. Here we have perhaps one of the main reasons for the victory of Darwinism even today, even though the accumulating evidence of science is steadily against the theory.[54]

But what if there is a legitimate scientific option to evolution which is not materialistic? For example, Yale Law School graduate Wendell R. Bird fully documents that the theory of "abrupt appearance" is entirely scientific, and that such a theory was capable of being advanced scientifically by scientists of an earlier era. Further, he shows that creation itself is not *necessarily* religious; it too can be fully scientific.[55]

2. A false theory can be accepted because scientific facts can be misinterpreted or forced to fit a theory.

The facts of the natural world are in the possession of every scientist, creationist or evolutionist. The issue in debate is the interpretation of those facts. Yet scientific facts may not only *seem* to fit a false theory, but scientific facts themselves may become irrelevant because of the intrinsic appeal of a particular paradigm whose own preservation becomes paramount:

> Yet no matter how convincing such disproofs [of evolution] might appear, no matter how contradictory and unreal much of the Darwinian framework might now seem to anyone not committed to its defense, as philosophers of science like Thomas Kuhn and Paul Feyerabend have pointed out, it is impossible to falsify theories *by reference to the facts* or indeed by any sort of rational or empirical argument. The history of science amply testifies to what Kuhn has termed "the priority of the paradigm" and provides many fascinating examples of the *extraordinary lengths* to which members of the scientific community will go to defend a theory just as long as it holds sufficient intrinsic appeal.[56]

The concept of phlogiston is an instructive example. The theory of phlogiston "assumed that all combustible bodies, including metals, contained a common material, phlogiston, which escaped on combustion but could be readily transferred from one body to another."[57]

Scientific experiments with zinc and phosphorus appeared to prove the phlogiston theory.[58] The concept was fully accepted for a hundred years and debated for another hundred years before it was finally disproven. But in fact, "The theory was a total misrepresentation of reality. Phlogiston did not even exist, and yet its existence was firmly believed and the theory adhered to rigidly for nearly 100 years throughout the 18th century."[59]

Awkward facts were cunningly assimilated, explained away, or ignored; it was the false theory itself which determined how science dealt with facts. The facts themselves had to bow to the "truth" of phlogiston; hardly anyone even bothered to consider an alternative theory. Thus, as time progressed and more discoveries were made which made it increasingly difficult to believe in phlogiston, the theory was not rejected but "was modified by the insertion of more and more unwarranted and *ad hoc* assumptions about the nature of phlogiston."[60]

In his *Origins of Modern Science*, Professor H. Butterfield observes how the phlogiston theory actually led to scientists being intellectually incapacitated to deal with the evidence:

> . . . the last two decades of the 18th century give one of the most spectacular proofs in history of the fact that able men who had the truth under their very noses, and possessed all the ingredients for the solution of the problem—the very men who had actually made the strategic discoveries—were incapacitated by the phlogiston theory from realising the implications of their own work.[61]

Denton comments, "It is not hard to find inversions of common sense in modern evolutionary thought which are strikingly reminiscent of the mental gymnastics of the phlogiston chemists. . . . The Darwinist, instead of questioning the orthodox framework as common sense would seem to dictate, attempts to justify his position by *ad hoc* proposals . . . which to the skeptic are self-apparent rationalizations to neutralize what is, on the face of it, hostile evidence."[62] Thus, the great many intractable scientific problems with modern evolutionary theory do *not* constitute a disproof of Darwinian claims but rather situations which require adjustment to the theory in order that the theory be preserved at all costs.

3. A false theory can be accepted because scientists assume the theory to be true only because of broad general support.

In the case of evolution, no one questions the basic theory because everyone accepts the basic theory:

> The fact that every journal, academic debate and popular discussion assumes the truth of Darwinian theory tends to reinforce its credibility enormously. This is bound to be so because, as sociologists of knowledge are at pains to point out, it is by conversation in the broadest sense of the word that our views and conceptions of reality are maintained and therefore the plausibility of any theory or world view is largely dependent upon the social support it receives rather than its empirical content or rational consistency. Thus all the pervasive affirmation of the validity of Darwinian theory has had the inevitable effect of raising its status to an impregnable axiom which could not even conceivably be wrong.[63]

Hence the constant refrain that evolution is a "undisputed scientific fact." Further, all disagreement with the current view becomes irrational by definition. As P. Feyerabend argues in his article "Problems of Empiricism" in *Beyond the Edge of Certainty*: "The myth is therefore of no objective relevance, it continues to exist solely as the result of the effort of the community of believers and of their leaders, be these now priests or Nobel Prize winners. Its 'success' is entirely manmade."[64]

4. A false theory can be accepted by scientists because they prefer its philosophical implications.

For example, there are many materialistic scientists who are also atheists and therefore more than happy to accept the atheistic implications of naturalistic evolution. Here, the very purpose of evolution is to explain things without recourse to God. Again, scientists are only men, and if the naturalistic bent of the human heart is an attempt to escape God, then evolution is certainly an appealing theory.

Many modern scientists have pointed out with seeming satisfaction that, given evolution, there is no need to consider God. This tends to make one suspect that some of these scientists may have ulterior motives for wanting evolution to be true.[65] For example, in his *Heredity, Race and Society*, Theodosius Dobzhansky observes, "Most people, however, greeted the scientific proof of this view [i.e., evolution] as a great *liberation from spiritual bondage*, and saw in it the promise of a better future."[66] As Aldous Huxley once confessed in his *Ends and Means*:

> I had motives for not wanting the world to have a meaning; consequently assumed that it had none, and was able without any difficulty to find satisfying reasons for this assumption.... The philosopher who finds no meaning in the world is not concerned exclusively with a problem in pure metaphysics; he is also concerned to prove that there is no valid reason why he personally should not do as he wants to do, or why his friends should not seize political power and govern in the way they find most advantageous to themselves.... For myself, as, no doubt, for most of my contemporaries, the philosophy of meaninglessness was essentially an instrument of liberation [sexual and political].[67]

8. What does probability theory say about evolution—and does this make evolution a "greater" miracle than creation?

The idea that everything has come from nothing is a bit hard to swallow, even for scientists. As modern science increasingly uncovers the indescribable complexity of the living world and simultaneously fails to explain the nature of abiogenesis (that life can originate from nonlife), the miraculous nature of all theories of origins seem to be made more apparent. In a sense, the term *miracle* is no longer properly restricted to only creationist ideology.

Nobel prize-winning biochemist Dr. Francis Crick commented, "An honest man, armed with all the knowledge available to us now, could only state that in some sense, the origin of life appears at the moment to be almost a miracle, so many are the conditions which would have had to have been satisfied to get it going."[68]

Hoyle's research partner, Chandra Wickramasinge, also noted, "Contrary to the popular notion that only creationism relies on the supernatural, evolutionism must as well, since the probabilities of random formation of life are so tiny as to require a 'miracle' for spontaneous generation tantamount to a theological argument."[69]

The esteemed Carl Sagan and other prominent scientists have estimated the chance of man evolving at roughly 1 chance in $10^{2,000,000,000}$.[70] This is a figure with two billion zeros after it and could be written out in about 20,000 booklets of this size. According to Borel's law, this is no chance at all. Indeed, this chance is so infinitely small it is not even conceivable. So, for argument's sake, let's take an infinitely more favorable view toward the chance that evolution might occur. What if the chances are only 1 in 10^{1000}? But even this figure is infinitely above Borel's single law of chance (1 chance in 10^{50})—beyond which, put simply, events never occur.[71]

Thus, in "Algorithms and the Neo-Darwinian Theory of Evolution," Marcel P. Schutzenberger of the University of Paris, France, calculated the probability of evolution based on mutation and natural selection. With many other noted scientists, he also concluded that it was "not conceivable" because the probability of a chance process accomplishing this is zero: "There is *no chance* (10^{-1000}) to see this mechanism appear spontaneously and, if it did, *even less* for it to remain. . . . Thus, to conclude, we believe there is a *considerable gap* in the neo-Darwinian Theory of evolution, and we believe this gap to be of such a nature that it *cannot be bridged within the current conception of biology*."[72]

Evolutionary scientists have called just 1 chance in 10^{15} "a virtual impossibility."[73] So, how can they believe in something that has far less than 1 chance in 10^{1000}? After all, how small is one chance in 10^{1000}? It's very small— 1 chance in 10^{12} is only one chance in a trillion.

We can also gauge the size of 1 in 10^{1000} (a figure with a thousand zeros) by considering the sample figure 10^{171}. How large is this figure? First, consider that the number of atoms in the period at the end of this sentence is approximately 3,000 trillion. Now, in 10^{171} years an amoeba could actually transport *all the atoms, one at a time*, in six hundred thousand, trillion, trillion, trillion, trillion, *universes* the size of ours, from one end of the universe to the other (assuming a distance of 30 *billion* light-years) going at the dismally slow traveling speed of *1 inch* every *15 billion years*.[74] Yet a figure of one chance in 10^{171} cannot even scratch the surface of one chance in 10^{1000}—the "chance" that life might supposedly evolve. Again we ask, who can believe in something whose odds are 1 chance in 10^{1000} to 1 chance in $10^{2,000,000,000}$?

If, for the purposes of argument, there are only two possible answers to the question of origins, then the disproving of one logically proves the other. If A or B are the only possible explanations of an event, and A is disproved, only B can be considered the cause. If the chances of evolution occurring are, for example, one in 10^{1000}, then the chance of creation occurring would seem to be its opposite—the odds being 99.9 (followed by 999 more 9's). Evolutionist George Wald of Harvard has stated that a 99.995 percent probability is "almost inevitable."[75] Then what of 99.999999999999999 (plus 985 more 9's)—the "chance" that creation has occurred?

Thus, it is not surprising to hear famous astronomer Sir Fred Hoyle concede that the chance that higher life forms might have emerged through evolutionary processes is comparable with the chance that a "tornado sweeping through a junk yard might assemble a Boeing 747 from the material therein."[76]

9. What do the factors of design and precision say about evolution?

The overwhelming evidence for design in creation explains why literally thousands of first-rate scientists remain either strict creationists or deists who accept that the universe can only be accounted for on the basis of a divine Creator.

Many scientists have rejected the argument from design as "fundamentally a metaphysical *a priori* concept, and therefore, scientifically unsound."[77] But this assessment is false: "On the contrary, the inference of design is a purely *a posteriori* induction based on a ruthlessly consistent application of the logic of analogy. The conclusion may have religious implications, but it does not depend on religious presuppositions."[78]

Indeed, the incredible complexity of every living thing offers compelling evidence that life could never have originated by chance processes.[79] Thus, wherever we look in nature, the hypothesis that things arose by chance flies in the face of everything we see before us:

> It is the sheer universality of perfection, the fact that everywhere we look, to whatever depth we look, we find an elegance and ingenuity of an absolutely transcending quality, which so mitigates against the idea of chance.... In practically every field of fundamental biological research, ever increasing levels of design and complexity are being revealed at an ever-accelerating rate.... To those who still dogmatically advocate

that all this new reality is a result of pure chance one can only reply, like Alice [in Wonderland], incredulous in the face of the contradictory logic of the Red Queen: "Alice laughed. 'There's no use trying,' she said. 'One can't believe impossible things.' 'I dare say you haven't had much practice,' said the Queen. 'When I was your age I did it for half an hour a day. Why sometimes I've believed as many as six impossible things before breakfast.'"[80]

The information content in the world's living creatures—animal, plant, and man—is infinitely beyond the libraries of a thousand worlds. A single amoeba's DNA alone has enough information storage capacity to house the entire *Encyclopedia Britannica* a thousand times over.[81] Yet in the good name of science we are asked to believe that such complexity arose by chance from absolutely nothing. It strains credulity to deduce that the infinitely more complex things of nature resulted from chance, when all the facts and evidence we possess concerning man-made objects state that these much simpler items *had* to result from intelligence, plan, and design. In other words, if the extremely "simple" items that men make, such as watches and computers, require—even demand—intelligence for their production, how then does the infinitely more complex world of nature arise by pure chance without any intelligence at all?

Consider a single cell. In his *Evolution: A Theory in Crisis*, molecular biologist Dr. Michael Denton discusses a small fraction of the complexity of a single cell. He argues, "Perhaps in no other area of modern biology is the challenge [to evolution] posed by the extreme complexity and ingenuity of biological adaptations more apparent than in the fascinating new molecular world of the cell."[82]

If we were to expand a single cell a billion times until it was 15 miles in diameter, then we would see something of its unmatched complexity and adaptive design.[83]

Even the most simple functional components of the cell, such as the protein molecules, would be revealed as highly organized and tremendously complex bits of molecular machinery. In whatever direction we looked there would be boundless numbers of these robot-like machines. We could see each molecule was made up of approximately 3,000 atoms arranged in highly organized three-dimensional spatial conformation. "We would wonder even more as we watch the strangely purposeful activities of these weird molecular machines, particularly when we realize that, despite all our accumulated knowledge of physics and chemistry, the task of designing one such molecular machine—that is one single functional protein molecule—would be completely beyond our capacity."[84] In other words, the complexity and information content of even "simple" *molecules* are so vast as to be unimaginable. In fact, to suppose that molecules of such complexity could have originated through any possible scheme of biological evolution is simply not credible: "Complex molecules that are essential to particular organisms often have such a vast information content as...to make the theory of evolution effectively impossible."[85]

Indeed, as we traveled about this gigantic cell, what we would be seeing is

> an object resembling an immense automated factory, a factory larger than a city and carrying out almost as many unique functions as all the manufacturing activities of man on earth. However, it would be a factory which would have one capacity not equaled in any of our own most advanced machines, for it would be capable of replicating its entire structure within a matter of a few hours. To witness such an act at a magnification of one thousand millions times would be an awe-inspiring spectacle.[86]

When we move from the cellular level to that of the human brain, the evolutionary scenario becomes even more implausible. Hardly anyone would deny that the human brain, weighing a mere three pounds, is the most complex structure in the universe. "Neurological and other specialized scientists have calculated that a space of 1.5×10^6 kilowatts of electrical power, 1×10^{21} wires, 1×10^{21} miniature tubes, and 2×10^{18} dollars in finances would be needed even crudely to simulate the human brain from the physiological viewpoint."[87]

The human brain consists of some ten billion nerve cells. Each one of these ten billion nerve cells exudes between ten thousand and one hundred thousand connecting fibers which enable it to make contact with other nerve cells in the brain. Thus, the total number of connections in the human brain is close to one million billion or 10^{15}.

> Even if only one hundredth of the connections in the brain were specifically organized, this would still represent a system containing a much greater number of

specific connections than in the entire communications network on earth. Because of the vast number of unique adaptive connections, to assemble an object remotely resembling the brain would take an eternity even applying the most sophisticated engineering techniques.[88]

To assume that such complexities in the cell and brain could arise entirely by chance is why some scientists are now referring to evolution as a myth—and even an affront to reason. Dr. Nils Heribert-Nilsson was a noted Swedish botanist and geneticist. Toward the end of his distinguished career he penned his magnum opus *Synthetische Artbildung* (synthetic speciation), an exhaustive treatment of more than 1,000 pages that was the culmination of a lifetime of scientific work and practical experimentation. His long years of experimental research taught him that the idea of evolution was "absolutely impossible," something more "at home in *Alice in Wonderland*." He finally concluded, "A close inspection discovers an empirical impossibility to be inherent in the idea of evolution."[89]

Robert E.D. Clark (Ph.D. organic chemistry, Cambridge University) comments in his *The Universe: Plan or Accident?* "The existence of design and nature is a fact which must certainly be taken seriously" because "in every main branch of science—physics, geophysics, astronomy, chemistry, biology—we are faced by the same surprising fact.... Nearly everywhere it [nature] shows the signs ... of something that we can only think of in terms of ingenuity and deliberate design."[90]

10. Are there scientists who believe evolution has hurt the cause of science?

Despite its monopoly on the scientific world, a significant number of noted scientists have felt that, whatever benefits it may have, the theory of evolution has also been harmful to the cause of science.

Dr. A.E. Wilder-Smith emphasizes that the "dead hand of Darwinism" has "weighed heavily on [scientific] progress for over one hundred years."[91] J.W. Fairbairn of the University of London asserts that evolutionary thinking has had "a deleterious effect on practical taxonomy."[92]

Dr. W.R. Thompson, the noted entomologist, in his introduction to the centenary edition of Darwin's *Origin of Species*, observed that Darwinism has had a wasteful influence in numerous scientific disciplines including genetics, biology, classification, and embryology.[93] He argued that because evolution had become an indefensible dogma to be defended at all costs, the cause of science itself had suffered:

> This situation, where scientific men rally to the defense of a doctrine they are unable to define scientifically, much less demonstrate with scientific rigour, attempting to maintain its credit with the public by the suppression of criticism and the elimination of difficulties, is abnormal and undesirable in science.[94]

World renowned Soviet biochemist and creationist Dr. Dmitri Kouznetsov, also with three earned doctorates in science, has further commented on the negative consequences of evolutionary thinking in science and other fields. He observes that in Russia, scientists usually "become creationists on scientific grounds" noting that "evolutionists are very subjective in which data they decide to use as evidence for their theory."[95]

After 40 years of scientific research attempting to prove the validity of evolutionary theory, Dr. Nilsson concluded that his time had been thoroughly wasted. He became convinced that the theory of evolution should be entirely abandoned as a serious obstruction to biological research:

> The final result of all my investigations and study, namely that the idea of evolution, tested by experiments in speciation and allied sciences, always leads to incredible contradictions and confusing consequences, on account of which the evolution theory ought to be entirely abandoned, will no doubt enrage many; and even more so my conclusion that the evolution theory can by no means be regarded as an innocuous natural philosophy, but that it is a serious obstruction to biological research. It obstructs— as has been repeatedly shown—the attainment of consistent results, even from uniform experimental material. For everything must ultimately be forced to fit this speculative theory. An exact biology cannot, therefore, be built up.[96]

Perhaps all of this is why another leading scientist, Dr. Louis Bounoure, Director of Research at the National Center of Scientific Research in France, once noted, "Evolution is a fairy tale for grown-ups. The theory has helped nothing in the progress of science. It is useless."[97]

11. Does evolution require as much faith as creationism?

Evolution does require faith. One can wade through hundreds of evolutionary textbooks and notice that although almost all are certain as to the alleged fact of evolution, all are equally uncertain when it comes to solid evidence for the *details* of evolution.[98] The problem is compounded because even though most specialists may be well aware of the problems in their own domain, they *assume* the evidence for evolution is well established in other fields. Yet it never is. This conclusion becomes evident when one examines the doubts that scientists have expressed in their own specialties concerning evolution.[99]

Thus, the modern theory of evolution has, in some respects, only replaced one religious faith (supernatural creation) for another religious faith (materialistic evolution). Few can logically deny that *both* theories require faith in the miraculous. As anthropologist Loren Eiseley observes in his *Immense Journey*, "After chiding the theologian for his reliance on myth and miracle, science found itself in the unenviable position of having to create a mythology of its own: namely, the assumption that what, after long effort, could not be proved to take place today had, in truth, taken place in the primeval past."[100]

What this boils down to is that evolution demands a personal choice—faith, if you will—to believe in natural processes rather than believe in what must logically be acknowledged as a far more credible option—creation by an infinite Designer.

Randy L. Wysong, D.V.M., an instructor in human anatomy and physiology, argues in *The Creation-Evolution Controversy*:

> Evolution can be thought of as sort of a magical religion. Magic is simply an effect without a cause, or at least a competent cause. "Chance," "time," and "nature" are the small gods enshrined at evolutionary temples. Yet these gods cannot explain the origin of life. These gods are impotent. Thus, evolution is left without competent cause and is, therefore, only a magical explanation for the existence of life....[101]

Thus, he points out that evolution itself requires faith:

> Evolution requires plenty of faith: a faith in L-proteins [lefthanded molecules] that defy chance formation; a faith in the formation of DNA codes which if

generated spontaneously would spell only pandemonium; a faith in a primitive environment that in reality would fiendishly devour any chemical precursors to life; a faith in experiments [on the origin of life] that prove nothing but the need for intelligence in the beginning; a faith in a primitive ocean that would not thicken but would only hopelessly dilute chemicals; a faith in natural laws including the laws of thermodynamics and biogenesis that actually deny the possibility for the spontaneous generation of life; a faith in future scientific revelations that when realized always seem to present more dilemmas to the evolutionists; faith in probabilities that treasonously tell two stories—one denying evolution, the other confirming the creator; faith in transformations that remain fixed; faith in mutations and natural selection that add to a double negative for evolution; faith in fossils that embarrassingly show fixity through time, [and] regular absence of transitional forms; ... a faith in time which proves only to promote degradation in the absence of mind; and faith in reductionism that ends up reducing the materialist arguments to zero and enforcing the need to invoke a supernatural creator.

The evolutionary religion is consistently inconsistent. Scientists rely upon the rational order of the universe to make accomplishments, yet the evolutionist tells us the rational universe had an irrational beginning from nothing. Due to lack of understanding about mechanisms and structure, science cannot even create a simple twig. Yet the evolutionary religion speaks with bold dogmaticism about the origin of life.[102]

Section Two
Science and Creationism

12. What is the real problem with a materialistic approach to science? Why can creationism be good science?

The problem with materialism is its inherent limitations which tend to skewer the interpretation of scientific data. The *bon mot* that evolution is "$1/10$ bad science and $9/10$ bad philosophy" has more truth to it than many scientists are willing to concede.

Evolutionary belief is deficient philosophically because it attempts to address the issue of origins on the basis of an inadequate approach. The issue is argued exclusively at the level of naturalism. It is forgotten that theology itself is a legitimate discipline of knowledge that should also be considered in the debate on origins. Approaching the issue of origins materialistically leaves too many major problems for explaining the data, data that everyone agrees is there. Thus, meaning or interpretation that is assigned on the premise of materialism alone will be deficient because the data is incapable of organizing itself adequately solely on this basis. This is why many scientists are currently unhappy with the nature of the case for evolution.

The components of science itself—classification, theory, experiment, etc.—reflect a framework of concepts which transcend scientific data. All attempts to explain or interpret are to some degree impositions on the data. So are attempts to disprove or disallow alternate explanations. In other words, because the data of science does not automatically organize itself, interpretive structures which themselves transcend the data must be imposed upon it. Again, the question is whether or not a solely materialistic structure is adequate.

We think that an approach that attempts to look at the data without a bias against larger theological implications is more productive. And there is nothing unscientific about this. The worldview of theism is just as adequate an explanatory framework for the scientific data as is the worldview of naturalism. For example, the data from science (thermodynamics, astronomy, etc.) clearly indicate a point of origin for the universe. Thus, "all the observable data" produced by astronomy indicate the universe was created at a point in time.[103] The data from science also confirm a high degree of complexity *throughout* the history of life and such complexity requires explanations which not only include but also transverse natural processes alone. (See Questions 8 and 9.) In addition, the data from science reveal an incredibly high degree of fine-tuning or balance within the structure of the universe at all levels. This also calls for an explanation that transcends natural processes and invokes the need for a supernatural Creator.

In other words, a compelling case from philosophy, logic, and science itself suggests that natural laws alone are woefully insufficient to account for the existence of the universe and the complexity of life that inhabits it. This becomes especially true when we consider the distinctive character of man, such as his abstract reasoning powers, moral sensibility, complex personality, spiritual nature, etc. Humans are so far removed from the level of animals that we simply cannot account for them on the basis of purely natural processes (cf., Mortimer Adler, *The Difference of Man and the Difference It Makes*).

The value of science is undeniable as a *part* of the larger picture explaining the world, but it cannot explain the entirety of that picture. Theism, in terms of its ability to explain a much larger range of data as well as the integration of data in other disciplines, actually offers a more coherent "big picture." Thus, when creation is affirmed in the context of theism, it meets the criteria of good science: It is testable, unified, and fruitful in a heuristic sense.

13. Is creationism religious only?

Is creation science really a science? Or is it simply a religion in disguise, designed to underhandedly put Genesis back into the school system? Although creationism is certainly a religious philosophy, it can also be a scientific doctrine, something attested to by many noted scientists and experts on the nature of the relationship between science and religion. For example, the volumes by Bird, Moreland (ed.), Geisler and Anderson, and Morris and Parker are only some of those demonstrating that creationism can be scientific.[104]

Dean H. Kenyon, professor of biology and coordinator of the general biology program at San Francisco State University, is one of America's leading non-evolutionary scientists and has a Ph.D. in biophysics from Stanford University.[105] A former evolutionist and coauthor of *Biochemical Predestination*, a standard work on the evolutionary origin of life, Kenyon now believes that the current situation where most consider creation science simply a religion in disguise "is regrettable and exhibits a degree of close-mindedness quite alien to the spirit of true scientific inquiry."[106] Kenyon is only one prominent scientist who has "extensively reviewed the scientific case for creation" and finds it legitimate.[107]

For example, in presenting the scientific evidence for the theory termed "abrupt appearance" (which incorporates relevant data from paleontology, morphology, information content, probability, genetics, comparative discontinuity, etc.), Bird observes, "These lines of evidence are affirmative in the sense that if true, they support the theory of abrupt appearance. They are not negative in the sense of merely identifying weaknesses of evolution.... The theory of abrupt appearance is scientific. It consists of the empirical evidence and scientific interpretation that is the content of this chapter. The theory of abrupt appearance also satisfies the various definitions of science...."[108]

Dr. Wilder-Smith also presents a scientific alternative to neo-Darwinism in his *Basis for a New Biology* and *Scientific Alternative to Neo-Darwinian Evolutionary Theory: Information Sources and Structures*.[109] The scientific case for creation is also ably marshaled by leading scientists in *Creation Hypothesis: Scientific Evidence for an Intelligent Designer*, J.P. Moreland, editor.

If scientific creationism is really religion masquerading as science (i.e., pseudoscience), and evolutionary theory alone is true science, why is it that literally thousands of first-rate scientists worldwide have abandoned evolution as a scientific theory and become *scientific* creationists? For so many reputable scientists to accept creationism as legitimately scientific means that evolutionists who claim it is only religion must be wrong.

Further, evolutionists have often claimed that no qualified scientist having academic Ph.D.'s from accredited institutions believes in creation. But those who argue in this manner are also wrong. Collectively, thousands of creationists have Ph.D's in all the sciences, some from the most prestigious universities in America and Europe. They have held honors, positions, and appointments that are equal to the best of their evolutionary colleagues. There are also thousands of non-creationist scientists who reject evolutionary theory, some of whom have also admitted that creationism can be scientific.

As one indication of the scientific nature of creation, consider the following comparisons of the predictions of creation (c) and evolution (e) with the scientific data:

Predictions: (c) eternal omnipotent Creator; (e) eternal matter [eternal matter is held by some; most scientists now accept the universe had a beginning].

Data: Universe began; matter degrades; life highly ordered.

Predictions: (c) natural laws and character of matter unchanging; (e) matter and laws evolve [held by some; most scientists believe laws are constant].

Data: laws constant; matter constant; no new laws.

Predictions: (c) trend toward degradation; (e) trend toward order.

Data: second law of thermodynamics.

Predictions: (c) creation of life the only possibility; (e) spontaneous generation.

Data: biochemical improbabilities.

Predictions: (c) life unique; (e) life-matter continuum.

Data: life-matter gap; biochemicals [not] formed naturally from nonlife.

Predictions: (c) life eternal; (e) life began.

Data: law of biogenesis.

Predictions: (c) basic categories of life unrelated; (e) all life related.

Data: law of biogenesis; reversion to type; fossil gaps; heterogeneity; similarities.

Predictions: (c) world catastrophe; (e) uniformity.

Data: fossils; sedimentary strata; frozen muck; present uniformity.

Predictions: (c) organs always complete; (e) gradual evolution of organs.

Data: organs always fully developed; natural selection culls.

Predictions: (c) mutations harmful; (e) mutations can improve.

Data: mutations vitiate; laws of information science.

Predictions: (c) language, art, and civilization sudden; (e) civilization gradual.

Data: archeology and anthropology show civilization sudden.

Predictions: (c) man unique; (e) man an animal.

Data: man-animal similarities; also gap—art, language, religion.

Predictions: (c) design manifest; (e) naturalism.

Data: life complex and highly ordered; natural syntheses.[110]

The above comparisons indicate that the scientific facts support the theory of creation more than they support evolution. Finally, if creationism is only a religion, why do evolutionists consistently lose their *scientific* debates to creationists?[111]

Perhaps this helps explain why polls indicate most people favor the idea of schools teaching the theory of creation in addition to the theory of evolution. This includes the vast majority of the national public (85 percent), two-thirds of lawyers nationally (who also find it constitutional), most university presidents at secular universities, and two-thirds of public school board members. One poll indicated 42 percent of public school biology teachers now apparently favor the theory of creation over the theory of evolution.[112]

14. Are there evolutionary scientists who say the evidence lies in favor of special creation?

Some evolutionists are frank enough to admit that special creation actually is the better theory, either in whole or part. Unfortunately, it seems that most scientists assume evolution has been proven in other fields and that their field of specialty is the only one with difficulties. For example, the botanist E.J.H. Corner of Cambridge University believes that evidence for evolution exists in certain other fields, although he admits to difficulty in finding evidence in his own field:

> Much evidence can be adduced in favor of the theory of evolution—from biology, bio-geography and paleontology, but I still think that, to the unprejudiced, the fossil record of plants is in favor of special creation.... Can you imagine how an orchid, a duck weed, and a palm have come from the same ancestry, and have we any evidence for this assumption? The evolutionist must be prepared with an answer, but I think that most would break down before an inquisition.[113]

Writing in the *Physics Bulletin* for May 1980, H.S. Lipson, of the University of Manchester Institute of Science and Technology and a Fellow of the Royal Society, confesses the following: "I have always been slightly suspicious of the theory of evolution because of its ability to account for *any*property of living beings (the long neck of the giraffe, for example). I have therefore tried to see whether biological discoveries over the last 30 years or so fit in with Darwin's theory. I do not think that they do."

He further concedes, "In the last 30 years we have learned a great deal about life processes (still a minute part of what there is to know!) and it seems to me to be only fair to see how the theory of evolution accommodates the new evidence. This is what we should demand of a purely physical theory. To my mind, the theory does not stand up at all. I shall take only one example—breathing." And he proceeds to show how one cannot account for breathing on evolutionary assumptions.

After further discussion, he asks, "How has living matter originated?" and concludes: "I think, however, that we must go further than this and admit that the *only* acceptable explanation is *creation*. I know that this is anathema to physicists, as indeed it is to me, but we must not reject a theory that we do not like if the experimental evidence supports it."[114]

In his *Biology, Zoology, and Genetics: Evolution Model Versus Creation Model 2*, Dr. A. Thompson observes, "Rather than supporting evolution, the breaks in the known fossil record support the creation of major groups with the possibility of some limited variation within each group."[115]

Dr. Austin Clark, the curator of paleontology at the Smithsonian Institution, observed in the *Quarterly Review of Biology*: "Thus so far as concerns the major groups of animals, the creationists seem to have the better of the argument."[116]

In the area of comparative biochemistry, Bird observes, "This comparative unrelatedness argument is an affirmative evidence for the theory of abrupt appearance, as not just Denton and Sermonti but Zihlman and Lowenstein acknowledge in reference to the comparative biochemistry evidence, saying that 'this constitutes a kind of "special creation" hypothesis.'"[117] Even such eminent scientists as Sir Fred Hoyle and Chandra Wickramasinghe, his research partner, in discussing the "theory that life was assembled by an [higher] intelligence" state, "Indeed, such a theory is so *obvious* that one wonders why it is not widely accepted as being self-evident. The reasons are psychological rather than scientific."[118]

Section Three

The Consequences and Implications of Evolutionary Theory

15. How has evolution influenced belief in God?

Mortimer J. Adler is one of the great modern thinkers. He is the author of such interesting books as *Ten Philosophical Mistakes* and *How to Think About God*, the editor for the *Encyclopedia Britannica*, and an architect and editor-in-chief for the 54-volume *The Great Books of the Western World* library. This set contains the writings of the most influential and greatest intellects and thinkers in Western history—from Aristotle to Shakespeare.

In Volume 1 of *Great Ideas: A Syntopicon of Great Books of the Western World*, Adler points out the crucial importance of the issue of God's existence to the greatest thinkers of the Western world: "In sheer quantity of references, as well as in variety, this is the largest chapter. The reason is obvious. *More consequences for thought and action follow from the affirmation or denial of God than from answering any other basic question.*"[119]

And here is where we see perhaps the greatest consequence of evolutionary theory—its denial of God and the unfortunate results which have flowed outward from this denial. As leading evolutionist Sir Julian Huxley once noted, "Darwinism removed the whole idea of God as the Creator of organisms from the sphere of rational discussion."[120]

Dr. Colin Brown received his doctorate degree for research done in nineteenth-century theology. Concerning the impact of evolution on Christianity, he confesses, "By far the most potent single factor to undermine popular belief in the existence of God in modern times is the evolutionary theory of Charles Darwin."[121]

Religion authority Dr. Huston Smith observes, "One reason education undoes belief [in God] is its teaching of evolution; Darwin's own drift from orthodoxy to agnosticism was symptomatic. Martin Lings is probably right in saying that 'more cases of loss of religious faith are to be traced to the theory of evolution... than to anything else.'"[122]

Newman Watts, a London journalist, observed, "In compiling my book, *Britain Without God*, I had to read a great deal of anti-religious literature. Two things impressed me. One was the tremendous amount of this literature available, and the other was the fact that every attack on the Christian faith made today has, as its basis, the doctrine of evolution."[123]

As a testimony to the religious impact of evolutionary thinking, consider the carefully drawn conclusions of the famous *Humanist Manifesto II*:

> We find insufficient evidence for belief in the existence of a supernatural; it is either meaningless or irrelevant to the question of the survival and fulfillment of the human race. As nontheists, we begin with humans, not God, nature, not deity.... We can discover no divine purpose or providence for the human species.... No deity will save us; we must save ourselves.... Promises of immortal salvation or fear of eternal damnation are both illusory and harmful.... Rather, science affirms that the human species is an emergence from natural evolutionary forces.... There is no credible evidence that life survives the death of the body.... We affirm that moral values derive their source from human experience. Ethics is autonomous and situational, needing no theological or ideological sanction.[124]

In light of the above, it should not surprise us if we find a logical relationship between naturalistic evolution and philosophical/practical atheism; indeed, this is made evident throughout atheist literature.[125] In *The American Atheist*, Richard Bozarth argues as follows:

> Evolution destroys utterly and finally the very reason Jesus' earthly life was supposedly made necessary. Destroy Adam and Eve and the original sin, and in the rubble, you will find the sorry remains of the son of god.... If Jesus was not the redeemer ... and this is what evolution means, then Christianity is nothing....[126]

Yet in spite of the harmful effects evolutionary thinking has had in regard to personal belief in God, it is new discoveries about the creation itself that are practically forcing modern scientists to reconsider God. As one example, we cite the text *Cosmos, Bios, Theos*, produced by 60 world-class scientists, including 24 Nobel prize winners. Coeditor and Yale University physicist Henry Margenau summarizes the logical conclusion for open-minded scientists as they face the incredible complexity and design of the universe they live in. Margenau reasons that there "is only one convincing answer" to explain the intricate complexity and laws of the universe—creation by an omniscient, omnipotent God.[127]

16. What are some of the personal philosophical implications of materialistic evolution?

In the evolutionary or materialistic worldview, man has no unique status other than which he may choose to give himself. As leading evolutionist George Gaylord Simpson observes,

> In the world of Darwin, man ... is in the fullest sense a part of nature and not apart from it. He is *akin*, not figuratively, but literally, *to every living thing, be it an amoeba, a tapeworm, a seaweed, an oak tree, or a monkey*—even though the degrees of relationship are different and we may feel less empathy for forty-second cousins like the tapeworm than for, comparatively speaking, brothers like the monkeys....[128]

According to naturalistic evolution, a trinity of basic factors have created the entire universe and all that lives within it—matter, time, and chance. Nobel prize-winning biologist Jacque Monod echoes the sentiments of many when he comments, "[Man] is alone in the universe's unfeeling immensity, out of which he emerged by chance...."[129]

As Cambridge scholar J.W. Burrow writes in his introduction to *Origin of Species*:

> Nature, according to Darwin, was the product of blind chance and a blind struggle, and man a lonely, intelligent mutation, scrambling with the brutes for his sustenance. To some the sense of loss was irrevocable; it was as if an umbilical cord had been cut, and men found themselves part of "a cold passionless universe." Unlike nature as conceived by the Greeks, the Enlightenment and the rationalist Christian tradition Darwinian nature held no clues for human conduct, no answers to human moral dilemmas.[130]

Therefore, as Monod concludes, for good or ill, "Our system of values is free for us to choose."[131]

Not surprisingly, in a universe so large and uncertain, millions of men ponder the meaning of their existence. When all is said and done, was there any real purpose in life? As Leslie Paul once observed, "No one knows what time, though it will be soon enough by astronomical clocks, the lonely planet will cool, all life will die, all mind will cease, and it will all be as if it had never happened. That, to be honest, is the goal to which evolution is traveling, that is the benevolent end of the furious living and furious dying. ... All life is no more than a match struck in the dark and blown out again. The final result ... is to deprive it completely of meaning."[132]

Whatever position we adopt, few would argue that the consequences are incidental. Indeed, our answer to the question of origins makes a great deal of difference. For example, consider just a few contrasts between the materialistic and Judeo-Christian worldviews:

Ultimate Reality

Materialistic view: Ultimate reality is impersonal matter. No God exists.

Christian view: Ultimate reality is an infinite, personal, loving God.

Universe

Materialistic view: The universe was created by chance events without ultimate purpose.

Christian view: The universe was lovingly created by God for a specific purpose.

Man

Materialistic view: Man is the product of impersonal time plus chance plus matter. As a result, no man has eternal value or dignity nor any meaning other than that which is subjectively derived.

Christian view: Man was created by God in His image and is loved by Him. Because of this, all men are endowed with eternal value and dignity. Their value is not derived ultimately from themselves, but from a source transcending themselves, God Himself.

Morality

Materialistic view: Morality is defined by the individual according to his own views and interests. Morality is ultimately relative because every person is the final authority for his own views.

Christian view: Morality is defined by God and immutable because it is inherently based on God's immutable character.

Afterlife

Materialistic view: The afterlife brings eternal annihilation (personal extinction) for everyone.

Christian view: The afterlife involves either eternal life with God (personal immortality) or eternal separation from Him (personal judgment).

Who would argue that such differences carry no meaning? To show that they do, we next offer one example.

17. What recent social and political consequences can be attributed to evolutionary belief?

As philosopher Will Durant once noted: "By offering evolution in place of God as a cause of history, Darwin removed the theological basis of the moral code of Christendom. And the moral code that has no fear of God is very shaky. That's the condition we are in.... I don't think man is capable yet of managing social order and individual decency without fear of some supernatural being overlooking him and able to punish him."[133] That Durant's assessment was correct can be seen all about us.

In a universe that is ultimately meaningless, what happens to individual and societal ethics? Why shouldn't the more powerful or more intelligent among us manipulate the less intelligent and powerful for whatever purposes they deem "good" and "worthy"?

Our century is replete with examples. The last 75 years have witnessed some of the greatest horrors of all human history—principally the result of Nazi and Communist atrocities. Nazi Germany was horrific, and Communism has been responsible for the death of approximately 25 times as many people as Hitler![134]

Nor have these ideologies been expunged. In Germany today neo-Nazism has become a powerful social force and neo-Fascism is rising in Italy—incredibly, under the leadership of Mussolini's own granddaughter. Despite the collapse of Communism in Europe and Russia, Marxist theory still rules over a billion people in China and other countries.

Nor can anyone be at all certain that Russia and Eastern Europe will retain their move toward democracy.

What does any of this have to do with naturalistic evolution? We noted earlier that evolution is based on the premise that time plus the impersonal (matter) plus chance formed all living things. In essence, man becomes something of a tragic accident, having no ultimate value, revolving at dizzying speeds through the dark corridors of space.

Unfortunately, philosophical worldviews molded by such thinking can easily find logical expression in the day-to-day living of millions of individuals. This was recognized by Sedgwick, a Cambridge geologist and acquaintance of Darwin, who felt that Darwin had shown every criminal how to justify his ways. He also believed that if Darwin's teachings were widely accepted, humanity "would suffer a damage that might brutalize it and sink the human race into a lower grade of degradation than any into which it has fallen since its written records tell us of its history."[135]

One of the greatest evolutionists of recent times was physical anthropologist Sir Arthur Keith. He devoted more time to studying evolutionary ethics than perhaps any of his contemporaries. His *Evolution and Ethics* illustrates that the ethics taught by Christianity and the ethics of evolution are not reconcilable: "Christ's teaching is . . . in direct opposition to the law of evolution" and, "Christian ethics are out of harmony with human nature and secretly antagonistic to Nature's scheme of evolution and ethics."[136]

Keith also understood that if we follow evolutionary ethics to their strict, logical conclusion, we must "abandon the hope of ever attaining a universal system of ethics" because "as we have just seen, the ways of national evolution, both in the past and in the present, are cruel, brutal, ruthless and without mercy."[137]

Indeed, when we examine the social and political influence of Darwinian theory in the latter half of the nineteenth and the entire twentieth century, the moral consequences are sometimes frightening. Keith himself observes the chilling impact of Darwinian theory upon Germany:

> We see Hitler devoutly convinced that evolution produces the only real basis for a national policy. . . . The means he adopted to secure the destiny of his race and people were organized slaughter, which has drenched Europe in blood. . . . Such conduct is highly immoral as measured by every scale of ethics, yet Germany justifies it; it is consonant with tribal or evolutionary

morality. Germany has reverted to the tribal past, and is demonstrating to the world, in their naked veracity, the methods of evolution....[138]

In Germany, Hitler saw in evolutionary theory the "scientific" justification for his personal views: "There is no question that evolutionism was basic in all Nazi thought, from beginning to end. Yet, it is a remarkable phenomenon how few are aware of this fact today."[139]

A form of Darwinism was also utilized effectively in the propagation of Communist ideology. Karl Marx "felt his own work to be the exact parallel of Darwin's" and he was so grateful that he wanted to dedicate a portion of *Das Kapital* to Darwin, who declined the honor.[140]

Marx wrote to Engels concerning the *Origin of Species* that this book "contains the basis in natural history for our views [of human history]."[141] In 1861 he also wrote, "Darwin's book is very important and serves me as a basis in natural selection for the class struggle in history...."[142]

Dr. A.E. Wilder-Smith remarks, "The political and anti-religious propaganda put out since Marx's time writhes with the most primitive Darwinism" observing that "it brutalizes those it is forced upon."[143] Marx's philosophy, like Hitler's, reflected the brutality of nature. He referred to "the disarming of the bourgeoisie...revolutionary terror ...and the creation of a revolutionary army...." Further, the revolutionary government would "have neither time nor opportunity for compassion or remorse. Its business is to terrorize its opponents into acquiescence. It must disarm antagonism by execution, imprisonment, forced labor, control of the press...."[144]

Given the impact of Hitler, Marx, and their associates, and the demonstrable connection of their antihuman philosophies to evolutionary atheism, the comments of historical philosopher John Koster are germane:

Many names have been cited beside that of Hitler to explain the Holocaust.

Oddly enough, Charles Darwin's is almost never among them. [Yet]...Darwin's and Huxley's picture of man's place in the universe prepared the way for the Holocaust....Hitler and Stalin between them murdered more innocent victims than had died in all the religious wars in mankind's history. They murdered these victims not with the misguided intentions of saving their souls or punishing their sins, but because they were competitors for food and obstacles to "evolutionary progress." Many humanitarians, Christian, Jewish, or agnostic, have understood the relationship between Nietzsche's ideas and Hitler's mass murder teams and crematoria. Few have traced the linkage back one step further to Darwin, the "scientist" who directly inspired Nietzsche's superman theory and the Nazi corollary that some people were subhuman. The evidence was all there—the term neo-Darwinism was openly used to describe Nazi racial theories. The expression "natural selection," as applied to human beings, turns up at the Wannsee Conference in the prime document of the Holocaust....

We can see the events of Hitler's Germany and of Stalin's Russia as a meaningless collection of atrocities which took place because Germans and Russians are terrible people, not like us at all. Or we can realize that imposing the life-is-pathology theories of Huxley and Darwin, of clinical depression masquerading as science, played a critical role in the age of atrocities. And we can take warning. People have to learn to stop thinking of other people as machines and learn to think of them as men and women possessed of souls....[145]

18. How has evolution influenced the interpretation of the Bible? What does the Bible teach about origins?

Evolution has influenced the Bible through the many theories proposed in an attempt to harmonize the theory of evolution with biblical teaching.

One such theory is called "theistic evolution." This is the idea that God supposedly used the gradual process of evolution to create all life, including man. Another idea is the "Day Age" theory wherein the days of Genesis 1 become vast geological ages, usually in which to insert evolution. A third teaching is the "Gap" theory which assumes a major chronological gap between verses 2 and 3 of Genesis 1 wherein the billions of years of evolutionary progress are inserted. Thus, all these ideas accept the fact of evolution by allowing billions of years for it to occur. A fourth theory is called "progressive creation," and it accepts long periods of evolution interspersed by creative bursts of divine activity to sustain the process.

We have studied each of these theories in detail and believe they all have fatal biblical flaws.[146] Attempts at accommodation fail because evolutionary belief and biblical teaching are only compatible at the expense of biblical authority. As *The Encyclopedia of Philosophy* points out, "It hardly needs saying that Darwinism is incompatible with any literal construction put on either the Old Testament or the New Testament."[147]

Perhaps if we show why evolution and biblical teaching are incompatible, we can see that theories which attempt to harmonize them, however well-intentioned, are doing a disservice. For example, if evolution is true, Moses was certainly in error when he wrote the creation account of Genesis. Thus, in order to "accommodate" evolution, harmonizing theories usually impose a figurative or non-literal interpretation on Genesis 1–2. But more than a dozen other biblical books also interpret Genesis literally. They, too, are implicated with error for falsely interpreting the book of Genesis.[148]

It is always a mistake to interpret Scripture in light of dubious theories, scientific or otherwise. Properly interpreted, Scripture will never conflict with any fact of science simply because God is its author. After all, God not only inspired Scripture, He made the creation itself.

Nevertheless, consider a few examples of how these theories raise more problems than they solve.

Genesis 1–2: God created the entire universe, its flora, fauna, and our first parents, in six literal days. Lexical, grammatical, contextual, and hermeneutical considerations do not reasonably permit the "days" *of Genesis 1* to be vast periods of geologic ages, as indicated, for example, by the commentaries on Genesis 1 of such Old Testament scholars as Keil, Delitzsch, Leupold, and Young.[149] (See Exodus 20:8-11; 31:17).

Genesis 1:27: God created man and woman directly on the sixth day of creation. But if evolution is true, God created men and women indirectly after billions of years.

Genesis 1:31: God pronounced everything He created, including man, "very good." But if evolution is true, God pronounced millions of years of human sin and death, "very good" (cf. Romans 6:23; 1 Corinthians 15:26).

Psalm 148:5: Creation is by instantaneous divine fiat, not millions of years of gradual evolution (cf. Genesis 1:3, 11,14,20,24).

Matthew 19:4,5: Jesus taught that God made man and woman "*at the beginning.*" This is an indisputable reference to Adam and Eve in the Garden of Eden. But if evolution is true, men and women would have appeared extremely late on the evolutionary time scale—not "at the beginning" (cf. Genesis 1:1; 2 Peter 3:4).

Romans 5:12-14; 1 Corinthians 15:21,22: Sin and death entered through Adam. But if evolution is true, sin and death had also existed for hundreds of thousands of years prior to Adam (cf. Romans 6:23).

Jesus Himself accepted divine creation (Mark 13:19); Adam, Eve, and Abel (Matthew 19:4,5; Luke 11:50,51); and Noah's Flood (Matthew 24:37-39; Luke 17:26,27). For Christians, at least His authority is supreme. The bottom line is this: If evolution is true, the Bible, literally interpreted, cannot be true and therefore cannot be considered reliable, let alone the Word of God. Conversely, if the Bible is God's Word, then it is evolution which cannot be true.

Conclusion and a Personal Word

In many ways, no issue is of more fundamental importance than the topic of origins. Has man evolved, or is he the creation of a personal God who loves and cares for him? The answer to this question doesn't just determine the choices one makes in this life. From a biblical perspective, nothing could be more unfortunate than to enter *eternity* having a mistaken view of reality. The good news is that it is possible for you to know God the Creator personally (John 1:1-3). You can do this through His Son Jesus Christ by sincerely praying the following prayer:

> Dear God: I acknowledge my sin and ask You to forgive me. I recognize that You have dealt with my sins when Jesus died on the cross for me. I ask Jesus to enter my life and be my Lord and Savior. From this moment forward, I believe on Jesus Christ who rose from the dead and is living now. I place all my trust in Him to be my Savior and Lord and to give me His eternal life. Help me now to trust You, live for You, and honor You with my life. Amen.

Receiving Christ as one's Savior is a serious commitment. Please contact a local church where Jesus Christ is honored or the Ankerberg Ministry in care of this publisher for helpful information on living the Christian life.

Notes

* Starred references are recommended reading.

1. Ernst Mayr, "The Nature of the Darwinian Revolution," *Science,* Vol. 176 (June 2, 1972), 981.
2. James Moore, *Darwin: The Life of a Tormented Evolutionist* (New York: Warner, 1991), xxi.
*3. W.R. Bird, *The Origin of Species Revisited: The Theories of Evolution and of Abrupt Appearance,* Vol. 1 (New York: Philosophical Library, Inc., 1989), 1.
4. Theodosius Dobzhansky, *Mankind Evolving: The Evolution of the Human Species* (New York: Bantam, 1970), 1.
5. Ibid., xi.
*6. Michael Denton, *Evolution: A Theory in Crisis* (Bethesda, MD: Adler and Adler, 1986), 358.
7. Ibid.
8. In Henry Morris, *The Long War Against God: The History and Impact of the Creation/Evolution Conflict* (Grand Rapids, MI: Baker, 1989), 112, citing Julian Huxley, "Evolution and Genetics," in *What Is Science?* J.R. Newman, ed. (New York: Simon & Schuster, 1955), 278.
9. Theodosius Dobzhansky, "Changing Man," *Science,* Vol. 155 (Jan. 27, 1967), 409, from Morris, *The Long War,* 20.
10. Ernst Mayr, "Evolution," *Scientific American,* Vol. 239 (Sep. 1978), 47, from Morris, *The Long War,* 20.
11. Rene Dubos, "Humanistic Biology," *American Scientist,* Vol. 53 (Mar. 1965), 6, from Morris, *The Long War,* 21.
12. Julian Huxley, "A New World Vision," *The Humanist* (Mar./Apr. 1979), 35-36, from Morris, *The Long War,* 19.
13. Kristin Murphy, "United Nation's Robert Muller—A Vision of Global Spirituality," *The Movement Newspaper* (Sep. 1983), 10, from Elliott Miller, "The New Myth," *Foreword* (Winter 1966), 1, from Morris, *The Long War,* 19.
14. Letter to Asa Gray, Nov. 29, 1859, in Francis Darwin, *More Letters of Charles Darwin,* Vol. 1 (London: Murray, 1903), 126, from David L. Hull, *Darwin and His Critics: The Reception of Darwin's Theory of Evolution by the Scientific Community* (Cambridge, MA: Harvard University Press, 1974), 9.
*15. See Robert E.D. Clark, *Darwin: Before and After* (Chicago: Moody, 1967), passim, and Moore, *Darwin,* passim.
*16. See Robert T. Clark, James D. Bales, *Why Scientists Accept Evolution* (Grand Rapids, MI: Baker, 1976), 37-42, 145, citing "The Devil's Gospel," Francis Darwin, *The Life and Letters of Charles Darwin,* Vol. 2, 124.
17. Charles Darwin, J.W. Burrow, ed., *The Origin of Species* (Baltimore: Penguin Books, 1974), 205, 230, 123, 227, 292, 453, 315-16, 217, 66, 215; Bird, *Origin of Species Revisited,* Vol. 1, 75; Clark and Bales, *Why Scientists Accept Evolution,* 36.
18. Hull, *Darwin and His Critics,* 3, 6, 14, 157-58, 169, 193, 208-09, 230-31, 263, 267, 275, 302, 338, 340, 343-44, 227, 139-49, 436, 32, and Denton, *Evolution,* 69; Burrow, ed., *Origin of Species,* I; Carlton J.H. Hayes, *A Generation of Materialism—1871-1900* (New York: Harper & Row, 1963); Clark, *Darwin Before and After,* 63.
19. E.g., Cynthia Eagle Russett, *Darwin in America: The Intellectual Response 1865-1912* (San Francisco: W.H. Freeman & Co., 1976), 216-17.
20. Cf., Bird, *Origin of Species Revisited,* passim.
21. Denton, *Evolution,* 345.
*22. J.P. Moreland, *Christianity and the Nature of Science: A Philosophical Investigation* (Grand Rapids, MI: Baker, 1989), 21.
23. Ibid., 21-42.
*24. R.L. Wysong, *The Creation/Evolution Controversy* (East Lansing, MI: Inquiry Press, 1976), 40-41.
25. Ibid., 44.
*26. A.E. Wilder-Smith, *The Natural Sciences Know Nothing of Evolution* (San Diego: Master Books, 1981), 133.
27. Clark and Bales, *Why Scientists Accept Evolution,* 29-95.
28. Pierre-Paul Grasse, *Evolution of Living Organisms: Evidence for a New Theory of Transformation* (New York: Academic Press, 1977), 3, emphasis added.
29. Cited in Bird, *Origin of Species Revisited,* Vol. 1, 141.
30. Dobzhansky, *Mankind Evolving,* 5-6, emphasis added.
31. George Gaylord Simpson, *The Meaning of Evolution* (New York: Bantam, 1971), 4-5, emphasis added.
32. Carl Sagan, *Cosmos* (New York: Random House, 1980), 27, emphasis added.
33. Morris, *The Long War,* 32.
34. Arthur Custance, "Evolution: An Irrational Faith" in *Evolution or Creation? Vol. 4— The Doorway Papers* (Grand Rapids, MI: Zondervan, 1976), 173-74.

46

35. Ibid., 174-75.

36. Ibid., 179.

37. Rousas J. Rushdoony, *The Mythology of Science* (Nutley, NJ: Craig Press, 1968), 13.

38. Ibid.

*39. A.E. Wilder-Smith, *The Scientific Alternative to Neo-Darwinian Evolutionary Theory: Information, Sources and Structures* (Costa Mesa, CA: TWFP Publishers, 1987), iii-iv.

*40. Jerry Bergman, *The Criterion* (Richfield, MN: Onesimus Publishers, 1984), passim.

41. In Ibid., vii, viii.

42. Ibid., xi.

43. In Ibid., 7.

44. In Ibid.

45. Ibid., 28.

46. Wernher von Braun, preface in *Creation: Nature's Designs and Designer* (Mountain View, CA: Pacific Press, 1971), 6.

47. Clark and Bales, *Why Scientists Accept Evolution*, 94; cf., 55-56, 70-87.

48. Ibid., 91.

49. George Wald, "The Origin of Life," *Scientific American: The Physics and Chemistry of Life* (New York: Simon & Schuster, 1959), 9. Dr. Wald, of course, believes in evolution and proceeds to argue that time solves the problems inherent in the spontaneous generation of life: "Time itself performs the miracles" (p. 12). Obviously, since he believes spontaneous generation occurred, his use of the word *impossible* must be considered qualified.

50. Ibid., p. 5.

51. G. Fana, *Brain and Heart* (Oxford University Press, 1926), 41, from Clark and Bales, *Why Scientists Accept Evolution*, 89.

52. Louis T. More, *The Dogma of Evolution* (Princeton: Princeton University Press, 1925), 117, in Clark and Bales, *Why Scientists Accept Evolution*, 93.

53. Wilder-Smith, *The Scientific Alternative*, iv.

54. Ibid.

55. Bird, *Origin of Species Revisited*, Vols. 1 and 2; cf., Vol. 1, 45.

56. Denton, *Evolution*, 348, emphasis added.

57. Ibid.

58. Wilder-Smith, *Scientific Alternative*, I.

59. Denton, *Evolution*, 358.

60. Ibid.

61. H. Butterfield, *Origins of Modern Science* (1957), 199, cited in Denton, *Evolution*, 351.

62. Denton, *Evolution*, 351-52.

63. Ibid., 75.

64. P. Feyerabend, *Beyond the Edge of Certainty* (1965), 176, as cited in Denton, *Evolution*, 77.

65. Morris, *The Long War*, 109-20.

66. Wysong, *The Creation/Evolution Controversy*, 40, citing Dobzhansky, *Heredity, Race and Society* (1952), 63, emphasis added.

67. Aldous Huxley, *Ends and Means* (New York: Harper Brothers, 1937), 313, 315-16.

68. Francis Crick, *Life Itself: Its Origin and Nature* (New York: Simon & Schuster, 1981), 88.

69. Cited in Norman L. Geisler, *Creator in the Classroom—"Scopes 2": The 1981 Arkansas Creation/Evolution Trial* (Mieford, MI: Mott Media, 1982), 151.

70. Carl Sagan, F.H.C. Crick, L.M. Muchin in Carl Sagan, ed., *Communication with Extraterrestrial Intelligence* (CETI) (Cambridge, MA: MIT Press), 45-46.

71. Emile Borel, *Probabilities and Life* (New York: Dover, 1962), Chapters 1 and 3; Borel's cosmic limit of 10^{200} changes nothing.

72. Marcel P. Schutzenberger, "Algorithms and the Neo-Darwinian Theory of Evolution," in Paul S. Moorehead and Martin M. Kaplan, *Mathematical Challenges to the Neo-Darwinian Interpretation of Evolution* (Wistar Institute Symposium Monograph No. 5) (Philadelphia: The Wister Institute Press, 1967), 75; cf., Bird, Vol. 1, 79-80, 158-65.

73. J. Allen Hynek, Jacque Vallee, *The Edge of Reality* (Chicago: Henry Regenery, 1975), 157.

*74. James Coppedge, *Evolution: Possible or Impossible?* (Grand Rapids, MI: Zondervan, 1973), passim.

75. George Wald, *The Physics and Chemistry of Life* (New York: Simon & Schuster, 1955), 12.

76. Sir Fred Hoyle, "Hoyle on Evolution," *Nature*, Vol. 294 (Nov. 12, 1981), 105.

77. Denton, *Evolution*, 341.

78. Ibid.

79. Coppedge, *Evolution: Possible?* passim; Bird, *Origin of Species Revisited*, Vol. 1; Denton, *Evolution*, 308-27.

80. Denton, *Evolution*, 342.

81. Bird, *Origin of Species Revisited*, Vol. 1, 72.

82. Denton, *Evolution*, 328; cf., Lewis, Thomas, *The Lives of a Cell: Notes of a Biology Watcher* (New York: Viking Press, 1974).

83. Denton, *Evolution*, 328, passim.

84. Ibid., 329.

85. Bird, *Origin of Species Revisited*, Vol. 1, 71.

86. Denton, *Evolution*, 329.

87. Kevin C. McLeod, "Studying the Human Brain," *Creation Research Society Quarterly* (Sep. 1983), 75.

88. Denton, *Evolution*, 330-31.

89. Nils Heribert-Nilsson, *English Summary of Synthetische Artbildung (Synthetics Speciation)* (Victoria, British Columbia: Evolution Protest Movement, 1973), 1142-43, 1186.

90. Robert E.D. Clark, *The Universe: Plan or Accident?* (Grand Rapids, MI: Zondervan, 1972), 151, 181.

91. A.E. Wilder-Smith, *The Creation of Life: A Cybernetic Approach to Evolution* (Wheaton, IL: Harold Shaw, 1970), 244-45.

92. Cited in Coppedge, *Evolution: Possible?* 180.

93. Introduction by W.R. Thompson to Charles Darwin, *The Origin of Species* (New York: Dutton Every Man's Library, Series No. 811, 1959), xx-xxiii.

94. Ibid.

95. Carl Wieland, "Interview with Dr. Dmitri Kouznetsov," *Creation Ex Nihilo* (Australian), Vol. 14, No. 1, 34.

96. Nils Heribert-Nilsson, *Synthetische Artbildung Lund Sweden: C.W.K. Glerups* (1953), 11.

97. Louis Bounoure, *Le Monde et la Vie* (Oct. 1963), from Wysong, *Creation / Evolution*, 418; also in *The Advocate* (Australian) (Mar. 8, 1984), 17.

98. E.g., Bolton Davidheiser, *Evolution and Christian Faith* (Nutley, NJ: Presbyterian Reformed, 1969), 302-13.

99. E.g., Bird, *Origin of Species Revisited*, Vols. 1 and 2; Clark and Bales, *Why Scientists Accept Evolution*, 98-105.

100. Loren Eiseley, *The Immense Journey* (New York: Time, Inc., 1962), 144.

101. Wysong, *Creation / Evolution*, 418.

102. Ibid., 419; cf., Denton, *Evolution*, 308-44.

103. Roy Abraham Varghese, introduction in Henry Margenau and Roy Abraham Varghese, eds., *Cosmos, Bios, Theos: Scientists Reflect on Science, God, and the Origin of the Universe, Life, and Homo Sapiens* (LaSalle, IL: Open Court, 1992), 5.

*104. J.P. Moreland, ed., *Creation Hypothesis: Scientific Evidence for an Intelligent Designer* (Downers Grove, IL: InterVarsity, 1994); Bird, *Origin of Species Revisited*, passim; Norman L. Geisler, J. Kirby Anderson, *Origin Science: A Proposal for the Creation-Evolution Controversy* (Grand Rapids, MI: Baker, 1987); Henry M. Morris, Gary E. Parker, *What Is Creation Science?* (San Diego: Creation Life, 1982).

105. Bird, *Origin of Species Revisited*, Vol. 1, xvi.

106. In Morris and Parker, *What Is Creation Science?* III.

107. In Ibid., 3.

108. Bird, *Origin of Species Revisited*, Vol. 1, 44-45.

109. Wilder-Smith, *A Basis for a New Biology* and *The Scientific Alternative*, v.

110. Wysong, *Creation / Evolution*, 422.

111. Cf., *The Wall Street Journal* (June 15, 1979); Dennis Dubay, "Evolution Creation Debate," *Bioscience*, Vol. 30 (Jan. 1980), 4-5.

112. Bird, *Origin of Species Revisited*, Vol. 1, 8.

113. E.J.H. Corner, "Evolution" in Anna M. McLeod, L.S. Cobley, *Contemporary Botanical Thought* (Chicago, IL: Quadrangle, 1961), 97.

114. H.S. Lipson, "A Physicist Looks at Evolution," *Physics Bulletin*, Vol. 31, No. 4 (May 1980), 138. Article reproduced in full in *Creation Research Society Quarterly* (June 1981), 14, emphasis added.

115. A. Thompson, *Biology, Zoology and Genetics: Evolution Model Vesus Creation Model 2* (1983), 76, cited in Bird, *Origin of Species Revisited*, Vol. 1, 49.

116. Austin Clark, "Animal Evolution," *3 Quarterly Review of Biology*, 539, from Bird, *Origin of Species Revisited*, Vol. 1, 50.

117. Bird, *Origin of Species Revisited*, Vol. 1, 102.

118. Fred Hoyle, Chandara Wickramasinghe, *Evolution from Space* (London: J.M. Denton & Sons, 1981), 130.

119. Mortimer J. Adler, editor in chief, William Gorman, general editor, *The Great Ideas: A Syntopicon of Great Books of the Western World*, Vol. 1 (Chicago: Encyclopedia Britannica, 1952), 543.

120. In Sol Tax, ed., *Evolution After Darwin*, Vol. 3 (Chicago: University of Chicago Press, 1960), 45.

121. Colin Brown, *Philosophy and the Christian Faith* (Wheaton, IL: Tyndale, 1971), 147.

122. Huston Smith, *The Christian Century* (July 7-14, 1982), 755, citing *Studies in Comparative Religion* (Winter 1970).

48

123. Newman Watts, *Why Be an Ape?: Observations on Evolution* (London: Marshall, Morgan & Scott, Ltd., n.d.), 97.

124. *Humanist Manifesto II, The Humanist* (Sep./Oct. 1973), 4-9.

125. E.g., George H. Smith, *Atheism: The Case Against God* (Los Angeles: Nash, 1974), 112-13.

126. Richard Bozarth, *The American Atheist* (Sep. 1978), cited in Richard Bliss, "Evolution Versus Science," *Christian Herald* (July/Aug. 1985).

127. Henry Margenau, "The Laws of Nature Are Created by God" in *Cosmos, Bios, Theos,* Henry Margenau and Roy Abraham Varghese, eds. (LaSalle, IL: Open Court, 1992), 61.

128. George Gaylord Simpson, "The World into Which Darwin Led Us," *Science,* Vol. 131 (1960), 970, from Bird, *Origin of Species Revisited,* Vol. 1, 139.

129. In Theodore Roszak, *Where the Wasteland Ends,* 249, citing Monod, *Chance and Necessity* (New York: A.A. Knopf, 1971), 112.

130. J.W. Burrow, introduction in Charles Darwin, *The Origin of Species* (Baltimore: Penguin, 1974), 43.

131. Interview with Jacques Monod written by John C. Hess, *New York Times* (Mar. 15, 1971), 6, from Francis Schaeffer, *Back to Freedom and Dignity,* 13.

132. Leslie Paul, *The Annihilation of Man* (New York: Harcourt Brace, 1945), 154, from Arthur Custance, *Doorway Paper,* No. 29, "A Framework of History" (Ottowa, Canada: 1968), III.

133. Will Durant, "Are We in the Last Stage of a Pagan Period?" *Chicago Tribune,* Syndicate (Apr. 1980), from Morris, *The Long War,* 149.

134. Declassified KGB records; Aleksandr Solzhenitsyn, *Warning to the West* (New York: Farrar, Straus & Giroux, 1977), 129; Communist China deaths are put at more than 30 million by some estimates.

135. In Marshall and Sandra Hall, *The Truth* (Nutley, NJ: Craig Press, 1974), 100.

136. Sir Arthur Keith, *Evolution and Ethics* (New York: G.P. Putnam's Sons, 1947), 69-70.

137. Ibid., 15.

138. Ibid., 28-29, 230.

139. Morris, *The Long War,* 79; cf. Benno Muller-Hull, *Murderous Science: Elimination by Scientific Selection of Jews, Gypsies and Others in Germany 1933-1945* (New York: Oxford University Press, 1988) for documentation of the role played by German evolutionary scientists in Nazi racial policies.

140. Burrow, ed., *Origin of Species,* 45; Jacques Barzun, *Darwin, Marx, Wagner: Critique of a Heritage* (Garden City, NY: Doubleday, 1958), 8; cf. Q.V. "Darwinism," *Encyclopedia of Philosophy,* Vol. 2, 304.

141. In David Jorafsky, *Soviet Marxism and Natural Science* (New York: Columbia University Press, 1961), 12, from Morris, *The Long War,* 84.

142. Hall and Hall, *The Truth,* 139-40.

143. A.E. Wilder-Smith, *Man's Origin—Man's Destiny: A Critical Survey of the Principles of Evolution and Christianity* (Wheaton, IL: Harold Shaw, 1970), 192-95.

144. Hall and Hall, *The Truth,* 150-51, citing Harold J. Laski, *Karl Marx: An Essay* (London: The Fabian Society, 1925), 19, 39.

145. John P. Koster, Jr., *The Atheist Syndrome* (Brentwood, TN: Wolgemuth & Hyatt, 1989), 142, 187-89.

146. On theistic evolution, see Burt Thompson, *Theistic Evolution* (Shreveport, LA: Lambert, 1977); on the "Gap" theory, see Weston Fields, *Unformed and Unfilled: The Gap Theory* (Presbyterian and Reformed); in general see Nigel N. de S. Cameron, *Evolution and the Authority of the Bible* (Greenwood, SC: Attic Press, 1983); on the "Day Age" theory, see note 149; on "progressive creationism," see Marvin L. Lubenow, "Progressive Creationism: Is It a Biblical Option?" *Proceedings of the Third Creation-Science Conference* (Caldwell, ID: Bible Science Association, 1976) and Marvin L. Lubenow, *Bones of Contention: A Creationist Assessment of Human Fossils* (Grand Rapids, MI: Baker, 1992), chapter 20.

147. Morton O. Beckner in Paul Edwards, editor in chief, *The Encyclopedia of Philosophy,* Vol. 2 (New York: Macmillan, 1972), 304.

148. In *The Remarkable Birth of Planet Earth,* Appendix B, "Henry Morris Lists 77 New Testament References to Genesis 1-11."

149. E.g., Keil and Delitzsch, *Commentary on the Old Testament in Ten Volumes,* Vol. 1 (Grand Rapids, MI: Eerdmans, 1978), 51; H.C. Leupold, *Exposition of Genesis,* Vol. 1 (Grand Rapids, MI: Baker, 1978), 57-58.